at

the

foot

of

heaven

Star Song Publishing Group
A division of Jubilee Communications, Inc.
P.O. Box 150009
Nashville, Tennessee 37215

Printed in the United States of America,
First Printing, September 1994

Library of Congress Cataloging-in-Publication Data

Smith, Kevin Max.
At the foot of heaven / poetry by Kevin Max Smith;
paintings by Jimmy A.
p. cm.
ISBN 1-56233-1008 : $19.99
I. Jimmy A.   II. Title.
PS3569 . M5375544A92   1994
811 '.54—dc20   94-32254
CIP

1 2 3 4 5 6 7 8 9 10 – 98 97 96 95 94

# At the Foot of Heaven

a collaboration

Poetry by Kevin Max Smith
Paintings by Jimmy Abegg

## ROMANCE

Rachel

Secret Intrusion

Silent Repetitions*

You Know How

Of Dogs and Whistles

I Will Bring Fire to Thee

Two Obsessions (Paradise)*

Captured

Queen of the Nile

Desmond

The Gypsy and the Nightingale*

You Wave Me Away

## SPIRITUALITY

At the Foot of Heaven

Listening to Thieves

Gift Baby

Tree Climber

40 Days, 40 Nights (Water Circus)

The Angel That Would Be King

Eyes Have Not Seen

Purgatory

You Gave Me Away

# HUMANITY

T.V. Evangelist Is Seen and Not Heard

The Skeleton Closet (Mary's Room)

Subtle Boy

3 Blind Men

Sweet Little Girl

I Am Doubting You Again

Indian Runners

Hang Your Head (Little Preacher)

Endeavoring to Be Wild

Vanity[*]

Some Things Are Better Left Unsaid


# ETERNITY

Via Dolorosa

Jordan's Kiss and Then Some

Belial

As You Wish[*]

My Reoccurring Desert Dream

Awake at Night

Draw Nigh

Wilt Thou?

Only one body of literary work is perfection. Everything else is a fabrication of thought, a trickling down of the mind processes of man. That is not to say that inspired works cannot still be fulfilled—only the divine stand alone. I believe this book of poetry to be inspired by the Spirit of God, yet written by a fallible human spirit.

Reality. My life is a myriad of ever-changing, shape-shifting pathways, turning to bring me closer to my destiny. Along the way there are pit stops, pitfalls, and sometimes endless searches. But I know where the tunnel leads. I know what is on the other side and I accept the wilderness of earthbound living. WE live to die.

I search for heaven on earth at times, but end up only finding true peace in harmony with God. God is watching, accounting, laughing, loving, and caring for all of us. But never take for granted the hand of Judgment.

If we could but see it all,
past the tangible things,
if we could but
touch the open space
to see the horde of silent wings.

And in the darkness
hear a song
a song of ancient ages.
and catch a glimpse
of He who sat
in the middle of the angels.

Eyes have not seen
nor ears have heard.

romance

## RACHEL

She was just enough to taunt the moon to fall
And just enough to bounce it rapid like a ball

# SECRET INTRUSION

I wish for you
in an untitled moment
to break this curse
of unspoken enslavement.

I am faulted for much
but willing to seek atonement.
I would count every speck of sand
every bit of stardust to be with you.

But without a doubt,
because without trust there is no hope,
I have never in my life felt
more alone than I do now,
for I know what I need needs me not.

And if there is need, then it is unspoken.

Let me break down the temple walls
to let light so shine in.
I wish for you in an untitled moment
to hold my hand through
this flimsy veil of humanity.
I am faulted for much even in this
secret intrusion.

LOVE SOUGHT IS GOOD, BUT GIVEN UNSOUGHT IS BETTER.

— William Shakespeare

## SILENT REPETITIONS

My world has many sections
sealed to all but one
You enter them with thunder
as clouds part back the sun

My mind lays calm as moonlight
with pearls of frosted dreams
You gaze into my darkness
and claw to break the seams

My heart hears silent repetitions
that shield my inmost will
You move among them freely
with transparent hollow heels

My life has been suspended
on sentimental sighs
And these worlds (of two) so varied
are mirrors of just one

WHAT WE LOVE WE SHALL GROW TO RESEMBLE.
— St. Bernard of Clairvaux

IN THE TRIANGLE OF LOVE BETWEEN OURSELVES, GOD, AND OTHER PEOPLE, IS
FOUND THE SECRET OF EXISTENCE, AND THE BEST FORETASTE, I SUSPECT, THAT WE CAN
HAVE ON EARTH OF WHAT HEAVEN WILL PROBABLY BE LIKE.

Samuel M. Shoemaker

# YOU KNOW HOW

You know how to hold me
when in cold be
heat, in bitterness
so sweet, passively
discreet (you would be).

So when this winter pass me
by, be the summer
passing sigh and
nigh, we fly.

You know how to touch me
witness the sense
and no less, impressing me
hence in this present
so tense.

So now often you seek
to scold me
when I am boldly
often in struggle
with myself, constant
enfolding inwardly old.

You know how
and knowing now
you keep this vow. (you should)

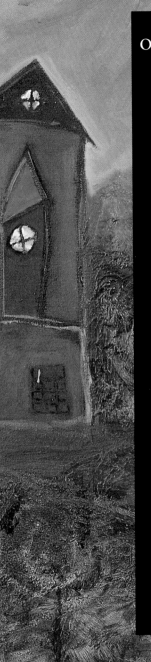

# OF DOGS AND WHISTLES

Like a burdened dog of
loyally ridden values
I follow you on

Like a trumpet played
by the seraphim of Heaven
I follow on

Like a comfortable beggar
in love with no surroundings
I follow you on

Like a train of iron will
constructed with no brakes
I follow

Like a performing seal
in dutiful fashion
I follow you on

Like grace-given virtue
in complete retroaction
I follow on

Like a bow on a string
in sync with conductor
I follow you on

Like the moon and the sun
in circular junction
I follow you on

THERE ARE THREE THINGS THAT ARE TOO AMAZING FOR ME, FOUR THAT I DO NOT
UNDERSTAND: THE WAY OF AN EAGLE IN THE SKY, THE WAY OF A SNAKE ON A ROCK, THE
WAY OF A SHIP ON THE HIGH SEAS, AND THE WAY OF A MAN WITH A MAIDEN.

*— Proverbs 30:18-19*

# I WILL BRING FIRE TO THEE

I will bring fire to thee
And you to me
Our souls intertwined
In relativity

I will bring fire to thee
And you to me
And all these nights ahead
No mystery

For you will
Throw away the keys
Which hold us dormant
In passages of futility

I will bring fire to thee
And you to me
And this passion ignited
Lofts heavenly

# TWO OBSESSIONS
## (Paradise)

There is a pool of
infinite blackness —
the edges crusted with
the smallest drops of sound

You draw from the pool
those saturated syllables
of mercy—the unspoken
words that sting of madness

Together we reach
into the maddening waters
to pull back the film
and see paradise

Lay your head
against my face
and search through
the brine to the
shiny bottom of faith

You then taste the
once bitter rawness
of purity and light
your mind then unravels
the cool, bubbling wisdom

When you leave my glance
and turn to follow fame
I see you in the fragments
of resonating speech

You believe man cannot
have two obsessions
no more than two souls
can form one heart

I now understand
you have one obsession
that feeds and burns
for solitude

# CAPTURED

I walk forever on this thought
of never having you
Its claim upon me is so
vehemently blue
the stars will not come out unless
you whisper on them coo

I will not leave this place
until I'm made a fool
Why does such a simple creature
have a hold on me
What is this cosmic power
that chains me to this solemn tree

Oh, how I wonder and I
blunder for the signet key
Her eyes they told me
Hands they sold me
Never to be free

WHATEVER YOUR HEART CLINGS TO AND CONFIDES IN, THAT IS REALLY YOUR GOD.
— Martin Luther

# QUEEN OF THE NILE

and darken all horizons
You hold me in this moment
a stamp upon my brow
A circle of loveless ambition

You dry up endless rivers
You level highest mountains
So tender wanton creature
and oblivious it slides

You hold me in this moment
entranced by so vague a movement
Your eyes betray a folding
of innocent intentions

Your hands, they hold the reins
Your hold is proven master
I sink into this cradle
of involuntary posture

Ignorant it caresses
For the tongue is swollen pride
Your kiss is forthright deadly

BUT NO MAN CAN TAME THE TONGUE. IT IS A RESTLESS EVIL, FULL OF DEADLY POISON.
— James 3:8

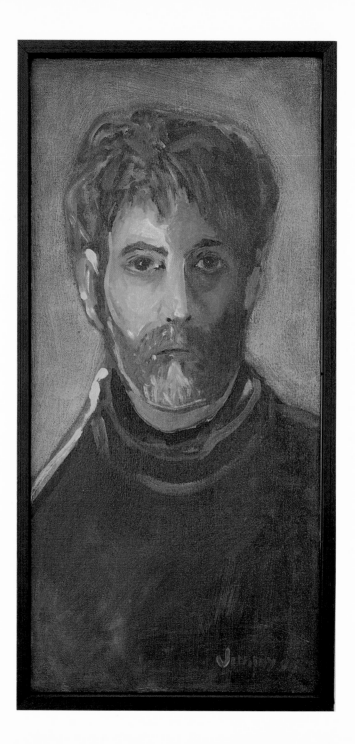

## DESMOND

Eyes that hold midnight
strange fascination
Smile that brings out light
my only placation

Creature if mortal
you hold all attention
If only to hold you
in blessed suspension

(or intention with)

# THE GYPSY AND THE NIGHTINGALE

THE LONELY HEART,
THE BURNING HEART
THE GYPSY MUSICAL
HOLD TENDERLY IN
WARM EMBRACE THE
LOVE OF HER NIGHT-
INGALE. HE TEASES HER
WITH FLIRTING PASSES
HE SPINS IN LOVING
DANCE SHE FILLS THE
AIR WITH SONGS OF
JOY HE WEAVES AN
AMAZING TRANCE. HE
ARCS HIS PATH TO
RUBY LIPS TIES CURLS
OF PASSION'S FIRE HER
HEART SEES THIS AS

PLAYFUL GAMES HE'S
FILLED WITH FALSE
DESIRE. SHE CAPTURES
HIM FOR ALL TO SEE
HER PRIZE OF LOVE SO
SAD HE BOWS HIS
HEAD IN MOURNFUL
TONES WHICH HAUNT
AND DRIVE HER MAD.
HER SEARCH FOR LOVE
DIGS DEEP EACH
TOUCH A PAINFUL
KNIFE FROM WOUNDS
SO DEEP OOZE PRE-
CIOUS BLOOD MIXED
WITH HIS INNER LIFE.
SO GO IN PEACE MY
LOVELY ONE HER
CRIES INTENSIFY HE
WINGS HIS FLIGHT TO
HEAVEN'S GATE HER
LOVE HELD DEEP INSIDE.

ARISE, MY DARLING, MY BEAUTIFUL ONE, AND COME WITH ME.

*— Song of Solomon 2:10*

THIS SORROW'S HEAVENLY, IT STRIKES WHERE IT DOTH LOVE.
— Shakespeare, *Othello*

# YOU WAVE ME AWAY

Alas, my love
you wave me away

In your tender smile
with eyes not following
you give me away
this night I weep
Tears of salt and blood

Alas, my love
you wave me away

Oh, so much time we
have given to accommodate
this doomed romance
Did you not know
to pray before the dawn?

Alas, my love
you wave me away

And I accept
this because of reality
that welcomes me back
You gave me away
because there was no longer
need for my petty excuses

Alas, my love
you wave me away

Your voice haunts me
deep in sleep at night
just before the sun breaks
through the blinds
I work my days
with an empty gutless soul
because I fear another chance
might break me furthermore

Alas, my love
You gave me away

Jimmy

*spirituality*

# AT THE FOOT OF HEAVEN

There are angels round my bed tonight
Some are there for comfort; some are there to fight

# LISTENING TO THIEVES

Three men hung crying (naked)
Rain spilling down
Through their feet
But one man spilled blood

Three men hung talking (naked)
One was groaning
The other searching
For the third man's
Knowing

Three men hung praying (naked)
One was cursing
The other pleading
And the third was
Calling out

Three men hung dying (naked)
One tasted fire
In his carcass wasted
The other was carried
By the third

JESUS ANSWERED HIM, "I TELL YOU THE TRUTH,
TODAY YOU WILL BE WITH ME IN PARADISE."

— *Luke 23:43*

NESTLED IN THE POOL

deep within

the comfort there beyond compare

To THE ANGRY world

lies far ahead

a brush of lov

and what lies not yet open

little King Hosannah

through the tunnel

stroke of creation

formed you

little one

and before you step

To seek your fate

they plan to crush you

with jealous hate

but little did they know the power you possessed

# TREE CLIMBER

Oh, little man
come down from that tree
Oh, little man
only one must suffer that fate

Oh, little man
only birds were made to nest
Oh, little man
tell me of your afflictions

Oh, little man
give me your numbered opinions
Oh, little man
tonight we walk right out of here

Oh, little man
if you have faith in the other
Oh, little man
short people are accepted there

Oh, little man
fetch me that glossy peach
Oh, little man
take up your tree and follow
me

# 40 DAYS, 40 NIGHTS
## (Water Circus)

These birds in hundreds
rain like pelt-like kamikaze
the day the heavens
caved in because of God's anger.

Man was floating
encircled in a boat made of pitch.
Fish were freed
to a place of utter mobility
and the screaming children
were swallowed up by the sea.

Inside the fortress
man smelled like the earth,
even though the earth
was not yet to be seen.

My curious cohorts
would play late in their pens of mud,
and furious others
clammered till they fell into sleep.

The old man's hand
was blood-soaked in teeth marks,
for the floating zoo
had no admission park.
And this lonely dove,
the soul of God in image,
found a twig
that set everyone off
in the
water circus.

PAIRS OF ALL CREATURES THAT HAVE THE BREATH OF LIFE IN THEM
CAME TO NOAH AND ENTERED THE ARK.

*— Genesis 7:15*

# THE ANGEL THAT WOULD BE KING

Morning light and he was there
Shimmering transcendence of everywhere
Broken halo of prideful lust
And glory in the farthest trusting soul

Keeper of the keys
Singsong of the heavenlies
Maker of his own divinity
Mephistopheles

Built his throne so all could see
Not far away from glory be
The angel that would be king they said
But late at night dethroned, unwed

Cast out amoung the bramble bush
To live in dark and grow his horns

SATAN, SO CALL HIM NOW, HIS FORMER NAME IS HEARD NO MORE IN HEAVEN.
— John Milton, *Paradise Lost*

# EYES HAVE NOT SEEN

Are there mysteries we should know?
can I find them in a book?
will science give us answers
to the questions we make up?

Oh, Lord have mercy on my soul,
my way this faithless sight,
how my mind bends for your law
in a world of constant plight.

If we could but see it all
past these tangible things,
if we could but touch the open space
to see the horde of silent wings

And in the darkness hear a song
a song of ancient ages
and catch a glimpse of He who sat
in the middle of the angels.

Eyes have not seen,
nor ears have heard.

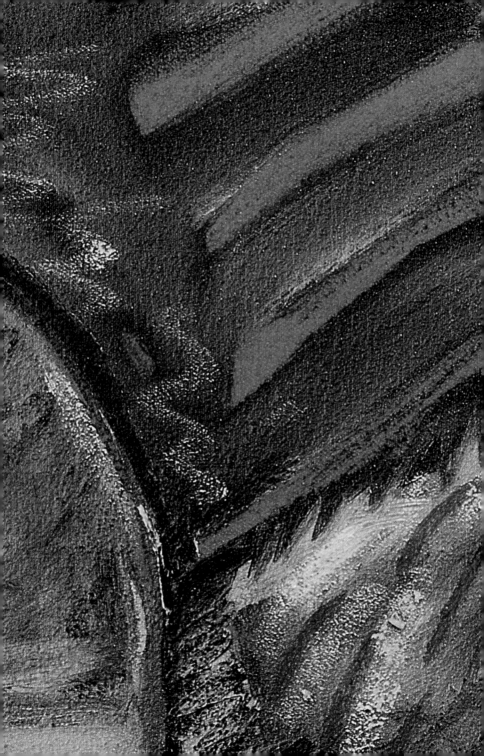

# PURGATORY

Shiver in my silk white robe
transparent but not quite
In all of this purity
there is still the presence of cold

Winter blast of noiseless
draft, of violated souls
Screaming down the hallway
right next door, almost too close

Oh these hollow doorways
leading up and down
Left then right, curving
round but never going outside

There is always an element
of confusion amidst
The well-scrubbed
walls of illusioned cleanliness
there was a fungus growing up
underneath

# YOU GAVE ME AWAY

ALAS, MY LOVE YOU WAVE ME AWAY IN YOUR TENDER SMILE WITH EYES NOT FOLLOWING YOU GIVE ME AWAY THIS NIGHT, I WEEP TEARS OF SALT AND BLOOD ALAS, MY LOVE YOU WAVE ME AWAY OH, SO MUCH TIME WE HAVE GIVEN TO ACCOM-MODATE THIS DOOMED ROMANCE DID YOU NOT KNOW TO PRAY BEFORE THE DAWN? ALAS, MY LOVE YOU WAVE ME AWAY, AND I ACCEPT THIS BECAUSE OF REALITY THAT WEL-COMES ME BACK YOU GAVE ME AWAY BECAUSE THERE WAS NO LONGER NEED FOR MY WORDS OF DEFAMED WISDOM HERE I SIT UPON A WOODEN CRUCIFIX MADE FOR ME ALAS, MY LOVE YOU WAVE ME AWAY MY LOVE WAS NOT ENOUGH WHILE STILL MY FATE IS STALKING IN JUSTICE IS MY CUP I HAVE SPENT MY DAYS WITH OUTSTRETCHED HANDS TO FASHION WOODEN SOULS, BUT ALAS, MY LOVE YOU GAVE ME AWAY AND WHY? GOD ONLY KNOWS

LIKE ONE FROM WHOM MEN HIDE THEIR FACES HE WAS DESPISED.
AND WE ESTEEMED HIM NOT.

*— Isaiah 53:3b*

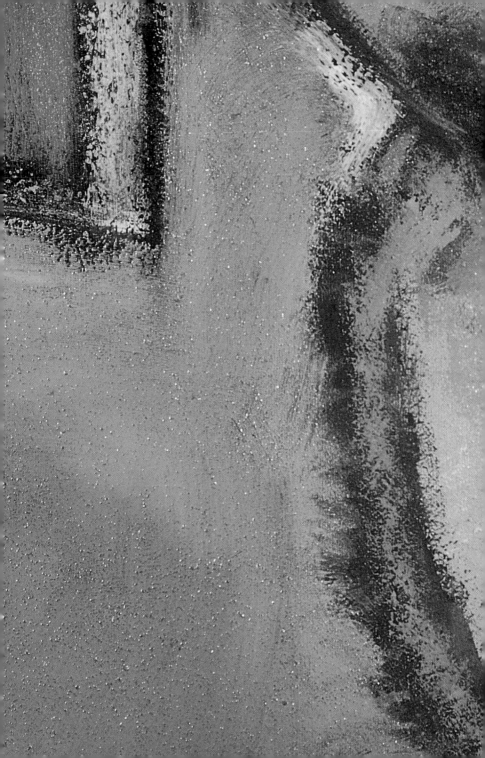

humanity

# T.V. EVANGELIST IS SEEN AND NOT HEARD

The man behind the dark shades smiled
He knew the way to reconcile

# THE SKELETON CLOSET

## (Mary's room)

The needle on the record
carves out another song
as Mary in her room alone
can't find her way back home

(she's not even playing
with a full deck any more)

The music keeps repeating
to another needle's score
she fills another hole
upon her arm so fair
and (on templates) her friendships
that never would be care

The melody is changing
as Mary finds seclusion
she's trying on a new dress
in the skeleton closet

# SUBTLE BOY

Brilliant eyes
and a nervous hand,
mark a subtle boy
all too well.

I could tell you more
but would hate to tell.
For then the mystery
would be open.
Like a jack-in-the-box
triggered and broken.

I love like a mother,
feel like a brother.
I'm a subtle boy
and sly as any other.

I AM A BEAST UNTIL I LOVE AS GOD DOTH LOVE.
—George MacDonald, *Diary of an Old Soul*

Fire puller leaned into it

## 3 BLIND MEN

Darkest bumble
Felt like crumble
Slightly mumble
That there's STAN

Smoking clover
Never sober
Smells like Rover
That there's JAKE

Thinks he's pretty
Says he's witty
Seeking pity
That there's FRANK.

THE WISE MAN HAS EYES IN HIS HEAD, WHILE THE FOOL WALKS IN THE DARKNESS.
*– Ecclesiastes 2:14a*

CHARM IS DECEPTIVE, AND BEAUTY IS FLEETING;
BUT A WOMAN WHO FEARS THE LORD IS TO BE PRAISED.

*— Proverbs 31:30*

# SWEET LITTLE GIRL

You're a cheap disguise
in your Sunday smile
You're an incurable wound
but a source of healing

You're my shadow of doubt
when I begin to believe
Your vanity descript
and entirely kissable

Christmas in the summer
Your habits impermissable,
umblemished in your beauty,
yet you scar my mind

Your allegience is fleeting
but I remain submissive
You live in deception
still, I would die for you

Sweet little girl

DOUBTS ARE THE ANTS IN THE PANTS OF FAITH. THEY KEEP IT AWAKE AND MOVING.
— Frederick Buechner, *Wishful Thinking*

# I AM DOUBTING YOU AGAIN

I am trapped in a room
of escalating grey
All appearances seem to blend
and mix together
I remember I have visited
this hall before

My stomach turns at the mention
of your lovely name
This smell is pungent
with a touch of heaven endured
My feet are planted strong
but my heart will run away

I am standing on a shore
of pallid green
shadows of many buildings
falling

# INDIAN RUNNERS

Ten little Indians
pulsed across the land
The barren desert
echoed their journey

I forgot how they ran
so fast but they did
Their feet not touching
the ground

Careful they were
not to step on bones
of their ancestors
even when the guns came
down around their heads

Across the horizon
you can still see them
running home

Breathless, beating rhythm
pulsed across the prairie
Ten little Indian
runners

# HANG YOUR HEAD

(little preacher)

Back behind the gospel shed

where the bookstore is still standing

behind the shelves of daily bread

you'll find him reprimanding

They said you were the "perfect" one

a shiny tin example

the man to get the job done

to build the new church steeple

But hang your head, lil' preacher

they found out you was cheatin'

but hang your head, lil' preacher

better practice whatchoo preachin'

P.S. God still loves you

FORGIVING IS LOVE'S TOUGHEST WORK,
AND LOVE'S BIGGEST RISK.

— Lewis Smedes

THE FOOL SAYS IN HIS HEART, "THERE IS NO GOD."
THEY ARE CORRUPT, AND THEIR WAYS
ARE VILE; THERE IS NO ONE WHO DOES GOOD.

— *Psalm 53:1*

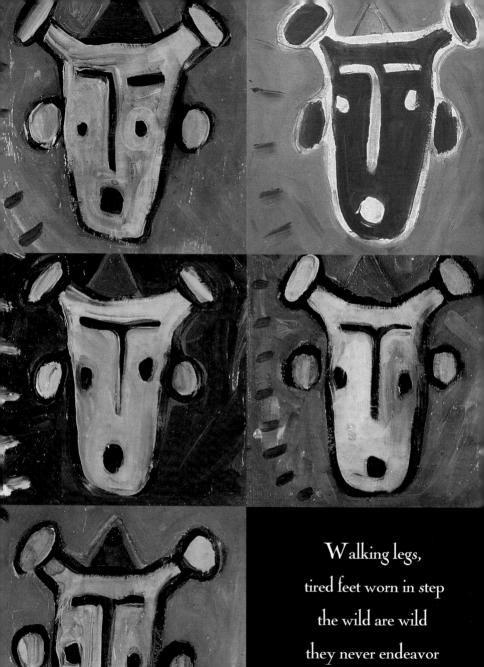

Walking legs,
tired feet worn in step
the wild are wild
they never endeavor
no pose is familiar
nothing new is twice.

The wild are wild
they never endeavor
they are made thorny, wild
unbridled and alone
born to be wildly overtaken
by vain pursuits.

A wild man will grow his hair wild
or shave it shocking complete
a wild woman will live alone,
breeding on others
the wild can fear as well
for they are  always in a
corner back kicked in.

Speed is their escape
and quick is their death and life
the only method to be wild is to
not care.

DO NOTHING OUT OF SELFISH AMBITION OR VAIN CONCEIT,
BUT IN HUMILITY CONSIDER OTHERS
BETTER THAN YOURSELVES.

— *Philippians 2:3*

Through crowds of familiar strangers
Your eyes pass over the room
You sort and dispose of needless souls
And smile but make no comment

You hang on each coy & cool comment
To complete the mask of control
You pierce each personality for food
And do all without comment

You gleam the source most like your own
And breed feelings of complete calm
An invisible hunger to feed and never want
You turn and leave without comment

Bodies of disbelief, sweet illusions of love
Lay scattered in your wake
The power of destruction hangs thick on air
Yet you still refuse to comment

Left with only simple shells of life
You push past the cries of wanting (passion)
Your thoughts move now to fertile landscapes
And you never turn to comment.

EACH HEART KNOWS ITS OWN BITTERNESS, AND NO ONE ELSE CAN SHARE ITS JOY.

— *Proverbs 14:10*

*Churchyard Yellow*

# SOME THINGS ARE BETTER LEFT UNSAID

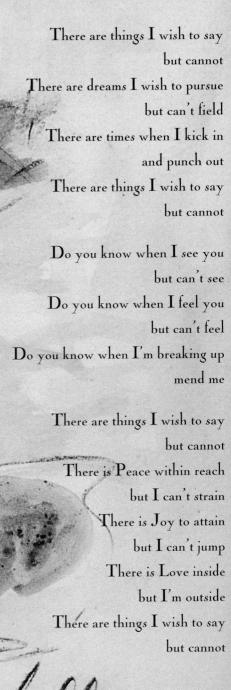

There are things I wish to say
but cannot
There are dreams I wish to pursue
but can't field
There are times when I kick in
and punch out
There are things I wish to say
but cannot

Do you know when I see you
but can't see
Do you know when I feel you
but can't feel
Do you know when I'm breaking up
mend me

There are things I wish to say
but cannot
There is Peace within reach
but I can't strain
There is Joy to attain
but I can't jump
There is Love inside
but I'm outside
There are things I wish to say
but cannot

with canon ball

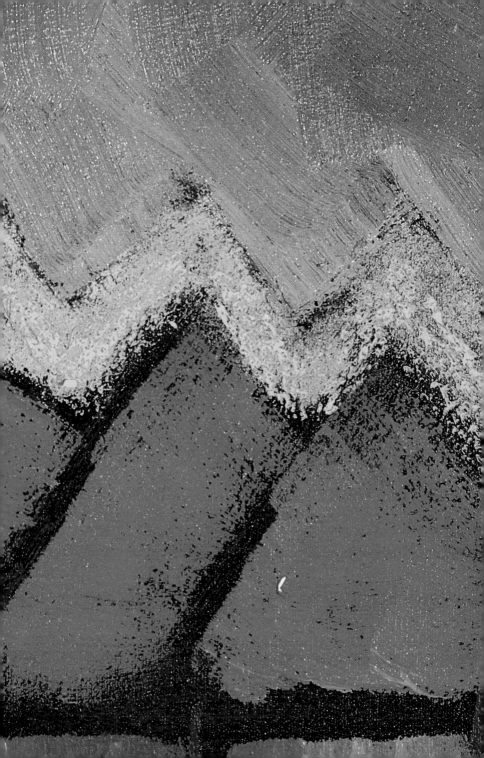

eternity

## VIA DOLOROSA

Procession of souls, grasp the hand of God
Find your purpose, on dirt which you trod

HE LIES IN WAIT NEAR THE VILLAGES, FROM AMBUSH HE MURDERS THE INNOCENT,
WATCHING IN SECRET FOR HIS VICTIMS.

— *Psalm 10:8*

# JORDAN'S KISS AND THEN SOME

WATCH THE
CHERRY PENNY
HANDED LOWLY
DOWN
TO THE MINOR
HUMAN LIVING
IN DISENCHANTED
REALITY NEVER
INTERPRETING THE
REASONS
OF WHY IT COMES
AROUND.

DANGER IS CLICK-
ING ITS
TEETH IN BAITED
BREATH
THE MINOR
SWALLOWS THE
PENNY
WHOLE, THINKING
OF SWEET
RELISH, SPARKLING
SUGAR
THEN THE
SENSATION COMES
LIKE A RUSH OF
SIN-FILLED SPASMS
CORRUPTED BY
THIS UNATURAL
POSITION OF
DREAMS.
THE MINOR SITS
DOWN FOREVER.

JORDAN'S MOTH-
ER CALLED THE
NEIGHBORS
FRANTICALLY
REACHING
JORDAN HADN'T
BEEN SEEN OR
FORECASTED
IN NOTIONS OF
GEOGRAPHY.
LITTLE TIMMY
SAID
"THE DEVIL'S GOT
HIM, MOM.
KISSED HIM LIKE A
FRIEND
THEN TOOK HIM
OUT,
AND THEN SOME."

THE PARLOR WAS
FILLED
WITH JORDAN'S
ONLY FRIENDS
THEY DIDN'T
EVEN
ACKNOWLEDGE
THE MAN
IN THE COAT WITH
THE WEATHERED
FACE BEHIND THE
BOX.

# BELIAL

YOU PIN ME
TO THE WALL
YOU PIN THE
TAIL ON ME
YOU STICK ME
WITH YOUR
WORDS
YOU PICK ME
WITH YOUR
NAILS

YOU CHOKE
ME WITH
YOUR PRIDE
YOU POKE ME
WITH YOUR
MIND

YOU WHIP ME
AS A CHILD
YOU TRIP ME
WITH YOUR
SMILE

YOU SEIZE
WITH IRRE-
SPONSIBILI-
TIES
YOU SQUEEZE
UNTIL I BLEED
STILL I OPEN
THE DOOR
WHEN YOU
KNOCK, I SAY,
"COME IN."

# AS YOU WISH

I must have made you whole
by thoughts dissected from wishes past
and yet you stand motionless
seeking comfort, fading fast

Sun kisses warm the chill of embrace
while dark arrows dart side and round
and flashes go to flashes fade
let thought of memories sound

or is confusion your art?

The haze of smiling melts
way the color blue
you know the next word
you let it fall from a broken smile

But before it sounds, I see
blue turn brass and
bells turn to sirens
of wails and distort your face

When impossibility makes itself known
and I remember
You have not fallen far
but stand behind my soul and say

I have forever kissed your face
I have always seen your smile
My heart knows your name in song
it is as you wish it to be

HELL IS THE ONLY PLACE OUTSIDE HEAVEN WHERE WE CAN BE SAFE
FROM THE DANGERS OF LOVE.

—C. S. Lewis, *The Four Loves*

WHEN THE LORD BROUGHT BACK THE CAPTIVES TO ZION,
WE WERE LIKE MEN WHO DREAMED. OUR MOUTHS WERE FILLED WITH LAUGHTER,
OUR TONGUES WITH SONGS OF JOY.

— *Psalm 126:1-2*

# MY REOCCURRING DESERT DREAM

The dancers came out at night
in the desert light
in ivory sandles
pounding a prance for me.

In my fever
I pitched dreams and tents of dark people
in white.

Silver and trim
of gold in their hands.
These dancers were so swift
and careful in the sand.

The women
eyes dark as the well
from which they drew their water,
seemed to call me and pull at me in
lamentations of their dead.

They brushed close
and then slipped away
into the dark.
The man inside of
the shadowed shawl
handed me the leathered
reins and said,
"Fetch me the moonlight when
she lets down her hair."

I rode out into the night so vast
in expansive wonder
all the time making music
of its own.

# AWAKE AT NIGHT

Tonight I wish to touch the stars.
To swing the moon in my cradle
To pull the sky around my neck
To embrace the night in its expanse

The sleeper has awakened to walk
through this universe of blackness.
No artist alone tonight
is left without a brush in hand

Dark, deep, haunted,
glorious throne rooms of night.
Angels fly from the nectar of pitch
black sky and heaven of starlight
Here I walk the silver strand
and throw my inhibitions
to the wind

Firmament of structure
God is holding
wire-tight circuitry of molding.
The heavenly host are alive tonight

There is no sandman, no grim reaper,
No boogey apparition or ghostly creeper.
In darkness there is only
absence of light
So turn
off the bedlight
tonight

HE DETERMINES THE NUMBER OF THE STARS AND CALLS THEM EACH BY NAME.

— *Psalm 147:4*

# DRAW NIGH

draw nigh
to me, you calloused beggar
draw nigh
and I will do the same
draw nigh
as the moon to the earth
draw nigh
and I will do the same
draw nigh
when your success is heavy
draw nigh
and I will draw nigh to you
draw nigh
when poverty reigns
draw nigh
and I will do the same
draw nigh
to me, you of swollen pride
draw nigh
and I will do the same
draw nigh
when the water covers up your soul
draw nigh

LET US DRAW NEAR TO GOD WITH A SINCERE HEART IN FULL ASSURANCE OF FAITH.
— *Hebrews 10:22a*

## WILT THOU?

Wilt thou
Wilt me
Wilting why
Words like
Whispers
Whisp like
Fly
Weeping
Willow
When we
Die
Wilt thou
Wilt me
Wilting why?

WHERE LOVE IS, GOD IS ALSO

~ Leo Tolstoy

KEVIN THANKS: JIMMY ABEGG, MICHELLE
ABEGG, ALEXIA, PIERETTE, JIMINA, DEB L.
RHODES, TOBY MCKEEHAN, MICHAEL TAIT,
DAN PITTS, LORI ANDERSON, GARY CHAPMAN,
RICK DENHAM, JODI MOORE, MEGAN
MACINTOSH, BEN PEARSON, BUDDY
JACKSON/JACKSON DESIGN, STAR SONG, MATT
PRICE, VELVET ROUSSEAU, BETH BARLEY,
CHRISTIENE CAROTHERS, CAPRILL CHAMPION,
JUAN OTERO, BONO, TEX COBB, STING,
MICHAEL GUIDO & FAMILY, MICHAEL
BLANTON, MARK TUCKER, NORMAN JEAN ROY,
AMANDA SAUER, DAN RUSSELL, LARRY
NORMAN, ALAYNA, BERNIE SHEAHAN, FRANK
OCKENFELS 3, KARI JOHNSON, OSCAR WILDE,
C. S. LEWIS, e. e. cummings, MARY SHELLY, EMILY
DICKENSON, BRENNAN MANNING, (ALL
THE PEOPLE OWNING AN ORIGINAL JIMMY
ABEGG PAINTING), BLUE SKY COURT, TIN
ANGEL, MAD PLATTER.

JIMMY A THANKS: KEVIN, GARY CHAPMAN,
MICHELLE MY WIFE, D. L. RHODES, BEN
PEARSON, MARK TUCKER, AND BUDDY. THIS
WOULDN'T EXIST WITHOUT YOUR HELP.

ART DIRECTION & DESIGN: BUDDY JACKSON/
JACKSON DESIGN, NASHVILLE • B/W COVER PHOTO:
PETER NASH • COLOR SLEEVE PHOTO: BEN PEARSON